H is for Horse

An Equestrian Alphabet

Written by Mike Ulmer and Illustrated by Gijsbert van Frankenhuyzen

I had so many helpful people for this book that it is important that I recognize them all. The love and respect they showed for their equine companions was clearly visible. Kelsee Foote and Sandy—my cover models, Jim Cloutier—farrier extraordinare with Elsie, the dog. Nathalie Trottier with Hobbie, Marge Bird, Susan Prorak, Candy Gerwatowski—owner of Red Creek Stables in Bath, Jane Heppner-Gamble with Hansel, Chelse Bonham and her mom with Darnell's Choice, Ethan Jarvis with Peanut the Pony, Robert Cable with Tripsee, Brianna Richardson with Lucy. And to those helping me with research, I'd like to thank Paula Hitzler and Emily Devers—Horse Teaching and Research—Michigan State University, Dan Fisher—Museum of Paleontology from the University of Michigan, Karen Waite—Animal Science Department from Michigan State University, the staff and horses from the Kentucky Horse Farm and all the gals at Potter Park's pony ride. Finally, sincere gratitude goes to Fred Derksen D.V.M.—Professor of Equine Medicine—Michigan State University. Your contribution was indispensable; from editing the manuscript and making suggestions on my paintings to helping me find my resources and posing with your own horse, Dutchess. You're a true Dutch friend, Fred. Thanks to you all.

—*Gijsbert van Frankenhuyzen*

Sleeping Bear Press
310 North Main Street, Suite 300
Chelsea, MI 48118
www.sleepingbearpress.com

© 2004 Thomson Gale, a part of the Thomson Corporation.

Thomson, Star Logo and Sleeping Bear Press are trademarks and Gale is a registered trademark used herein under license.

Printed and bound in Canada.

10 9 8 7 6 5 4 3 2 1

Library of Congress Cataloging-in-Publication Data

Ulmer, Michael, 1959-
H is for horse : an equestrian alphabet / written by Mike Ulmer ;
illustrated by Gijsbert van Frankenhuyzen.
p. cm.
ISBN 1-58536-213-1
1. Horses—Juvenile literature. 2. English language—Alphabet—
Juvenile literature. I. Frankenhuyzen, Gijsbert van, ill. II. Title.
SF302.U58 2004
428.1—dc22   2004005261

*This book is dedicated to my horse-loving daughter, Sadie Ulmer
and to Camilla Willings, Debbie Carson, Barb Bowen, Chris Firth-Eagland,
and all the people who helped us along our journey.*

MIKE

*I would like to dedicate this book to my nephew Tyler, and his
long-standing relationship with the horses in the Therapeutic Ride program.
Your strength and courage are an inspiration for us all.
And to every person and horse involved in that wonderful program.*

GIJSBERT

A is here to start the party.
It kicks off our horsey fun.
A's the first part of our journey
and of horses, second to none.
Be they Appies, be they Arabs

A a

Arabs, Akhal-Tekes, and Andalusians are purebred horses whose origins spread around the world. They are examples of horse breeds carefully managed to maintain their characteristics through generations. Breeds are a fun way to classify horses but a nonpurebred or "grade" horse, is just as likely to be a great partner.

Men and women, boys and girls all over the world love horses. There are 9 million horses in the United States today, 900,000 in Canada and as many as 60 million worldwide. Our love for horses goes beyond riding. In fact, many people keep horses strictly as companions.

nore credit
ll home
kest areas
zone,
ng sitting
he spit
ever say
st a bit.

The clatter of hooves and the swish of a tail
was the sound of the law on the old Western trail.
C is for Cavalry and the armies of men
who jumped on their horses when trouble began.
C stands for Canada and the mounted police
who brought law and order to the ranges and streets;
our frontier was settled, our statutes enforced
from a spot in the saddle, on the back of a horse.

The horse was instrumental in settling and bringing law and order to the western United States and western Canada. Canada's North-West Mounted Police were formed in 1873 and would later be renamed the Royal Canadian Mounted Police. Founded by Stephen Austin in 1823, the Texas Rangers would evolve into an elite crime-fighting organization.

C also stands for Comanche, one of the most famous horses in American history. Comanche was the only U.S. Army survivor of the massacre at Little Big Horn in 1876. He would outlive the man who rode him, Captain Myles Keogh, by 15 years.

Traveller and Little Sorrel were nearly as well known as the Confederate Generals who rode them, Robert E. Lee and Stonewall Jackson.

D is for the word Direction—
this might come as a surprise—
you can make your own selection
by the way you use your eyes.
Where you look is where you're heading.
Horses know how this is done,
so when you look where you are going,
know you're not the only one.

E e

Imagine if your mom could hear
each word you said, from far or near.
She'd have two Ears, just like your horse,
one pointing South, one heading North.
And every unkind word you said
would land you in trouble and up to bed.
Each day would carry fear and dread
if Mom had horse ears on her head.

Horses have much better hearing than we do and sometimes are startled by things we do not notice. Ears are also a great indicator of how a horse is feeling. If they are forward, the horse is eager or interested. Ears pinned back usually mean a horse is anxious or angry. One ear forward and back shows divided attention. When you lift a rein, notice how the horse flexes his ear on the same side you picked up. Your horse is using his ears to indicate he is noticing what you have done.

Here's the question I'm burdened with:
Why are Farriers all called Smith?
It seems to happen all the time
without reason and without rhyme.
On Sundays and vacation time
their own last name will work just fine.
But come Monday morning, at the stroke of six
everyone starts to call them Smith.

The farrier trims your horse's hooves and applies shoes. Most horse people use the word blacksmith as well as farrier, hence the use of the word 'Smith' or 'Smitty' for the farrier.

Like our finger and toenails, horse hooves grow continually. Depending on the time of year, a horse will need to be clipped or reshod every four to six weeks and that means at least a dozen shoe changes a year. Remember the horse owner's credo: no hoof, no horse.

F
f

G denotes the place that's best
    for putting bad horse habits to rest.
    G means Ground, and groundwork can
make better partners between horse and man.
    If you want to ride, not battle,
start on the ground and end in the saddle.
    If you try things the other way around,
don't be surprised when trouble's found.

A longe (pronounced lunge) line is a great way to exercise your horse. Many pleasure horses aren't worked enough to stay in excellent condition. Longing helps reinforce commands and opens up the lines of communication between the horse and rider before she gets in the saddle.

Veteran horse people consider ground manners an essential quality in a horse. A horse with good ground manners ties easily. He doesn't intrude on his handler's space when he is being walked or handled inside the stall or paddock. A horse with good ground manners does not resist having his halter put on or being put in crossties, and lifts his hoof for cleaning.

G g

Imagine a line your horse can't see
but she always knows it's there.
It shows what she's allowed to do
and when and how and where.
When it comes to horse and rider
there's a line your horse can't cross.
There must be belief inside her—
in this **H**erd you are the boss.

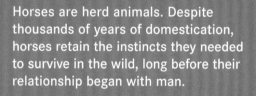

H h

Horses are herd animals. Despite thousands of years of domestication, horses retain the instincts they needed to survive in the wild, long before their relationship began with man.

In every herd, there is a boss. Your horse needs you to be the herd boss. That means you must build his respect for you by following through on commands and riding him properly. If a horse feels you are a poor herd boss, he will try to take the job for himself. The result will be a poor and even unsafe ride, and frustration for both horse and rider.

H also stands for hands. Hands is how a horse is measured. An adult horse that is 14 hands high is considered small. Draft breeds can go higher than 17 hands high.

I is for the words In harness.
They denote the special breeds.
Born for pulling and for plowing,
they once ruled the streets and fields.
Be they Clydesdales, be they Shires,
be they Friesians or Cleveland Bays,
they hauled milk and helped fight fires;
they were the engines of the olden days.

There're **J**udges scattered across the nation.
All are experts in horse conformation.
There're judges for your horse's walk;
they judge her canter, post, and trot.
There're judges for her color and breed.
They'll guide you on the proper lead.
There're judges for each show and ring.
There're judges for judging everything.

Judging horses is like judging beauty contests, only with more legs to study. In halter class, competitors bring their horses to be appraised by judges who study conformation, or how the horse is put together. Is a horse over at the knee? Are its feet splayed or its legs set too far out?

In dressage, judges note how well horse and rider combine for subtle movements inside a rectangular ring. Hunt seat judges monitor a rider's equitation or positioning as they compete over jumps or in 'flat' classes that don't involve jumps. Judges in the hunter's classes grade a horse's form as it jumps over fences.

J j

K

You can't have a horse without a kit. The kit contains currycombs, to loosen dirt and hair and remove lice eggs. Bot knives are used to remove botfly eggs. A dandy brush and a body brush bring the coat to a nice shine. You also need a pick, to clean the horse's hooves. Grooming helps you get close to your horse and gives you a chance to look for any cuts or injuries.

K also stands for the Kentucky Derby, the most prestigious thoroughbred horse race in the world. The Derby, the Belmont Stakes in New York State, and the Preakness in Baltimore, Maryland make up racing's Triple Crown.

Lexington, Kentucky is home of the world-famous Kentucky Horse Park. The park attracts 800,000 visitors a year and is the final resting place of one of the greatest of all thoroughbreds, the great Man o' War. With their spectacular athleticism and competitiveness, thoroughbreds have long dominated many forms of racing.

I've got a tool to catch a bot—
if I knew what they were, I'd catch a lot.
I've got a bag for my horse's tail.
I've just the tool for horseshoe nails.
I've got elastics for her braids.
K If I don't have it, it's not been made.
is for my bright red Kit.
I wonder what I did with it?

If you know your two-point stance,
if you favor riding boots,
if you know jodhpurs are pants,
if you know a horn won't toot,
if you keep your reins just right,
not too loose and not too tight,
if you know each single gait,
I'd say your Lessons are up-to-date.

M m

Mucking out a stall means removing manure and swapping wet bedding for fresh bedding. A horse will poo six to 10 times a day. If a horse is in a stall all day, that area should be mucked out at least twice. Horses need you to do the things they cannot. The bedding in a stall can be straw, sawdust, wood chips, peat moss or even crushed peanut shells. Remember to keep as much of the unsoiled bedding as possible, since throwing out good bedding with bad is a waste of money.

M is also for matriarch, the lead mare in a herd. The matriarch, not the herd stallion, is the boss. She usually operates ahead of the others and decides where the herd will graze and for how long.

One thing you should know for sure—
if you've got a horse, you've got **M**anure.
I thought that once, maybe twice a day
I'd grab a shovel; for the rest I'd play.
How hard could it be, I used to think,
to keep my horses free from stink.
Boy what a joke. Man, what a dream.
A horse is a manure-making machine.

N n

Somewhere between 8,000 and 11,000 years ago, horses became extinct in North and South America. The horse was not alone; in fact, a host of animals from the saber-toothed tiger to the woolly mammoth disappeared as well. While no one knows for sure why horses disappeared, the revival of the horse is more easily explained. Spanish explorers were the first to reintroduce horses to North America around 1519. It took more than two centuries for horses to become common again across the United States and Canada.

N is also for Northern Dancer, the king of the thoroughbred bloodlines. His offspring have won thousands of races worldwide.

Overo and Overall
   confuse me through and through—
one is dark with patches;
   the other one is too.
   One refers to the paint horse
kept in many barns.
   The other is a thing you wear
      while painting on the farm.

O is for Overo and overall. You ride an Overo horse. You wear overalls. There are dozens of variations of horse colors and markings. An Overo horse is a pinto or paint horse that has a dark coat with white patches. (My horse, Sky, is a paint with blue eyes.)

A bay horse is brown with a black mane and tail. A horse with a deep brown color is considered, naturally enough, a brown. A chestnut or sorrel-colored horse is reddish brown with a tail and mane of the same color. A roan's coat is a blend of white and colored hair.

Oo

There is a place where you can go
to learn about jumping and talk about shows
and how to groom, and comb a mane.
It's where first aid is well explained.
This lovely place is close for most—
there're 600 chapters from coast to coast.
Yes, Pony Club's the place to be.
It's my first choice for the letter P.

The United States Pony Club boasts 12,000 members in 48 clubs across the country. Pony Clubs are even more prevalent in Great Britain where 40,000 boys and girls participate. More than 137,000 children and young adults are members of Pony Club worldwide. Not all members have horses although, to belong, members should have some access to a horse. Horses of all breeds, not just ponies and pony-sized horses, are discussed at Pony Club.

Another great place to learn about horses in Canada and the United States is your local 4-H club.

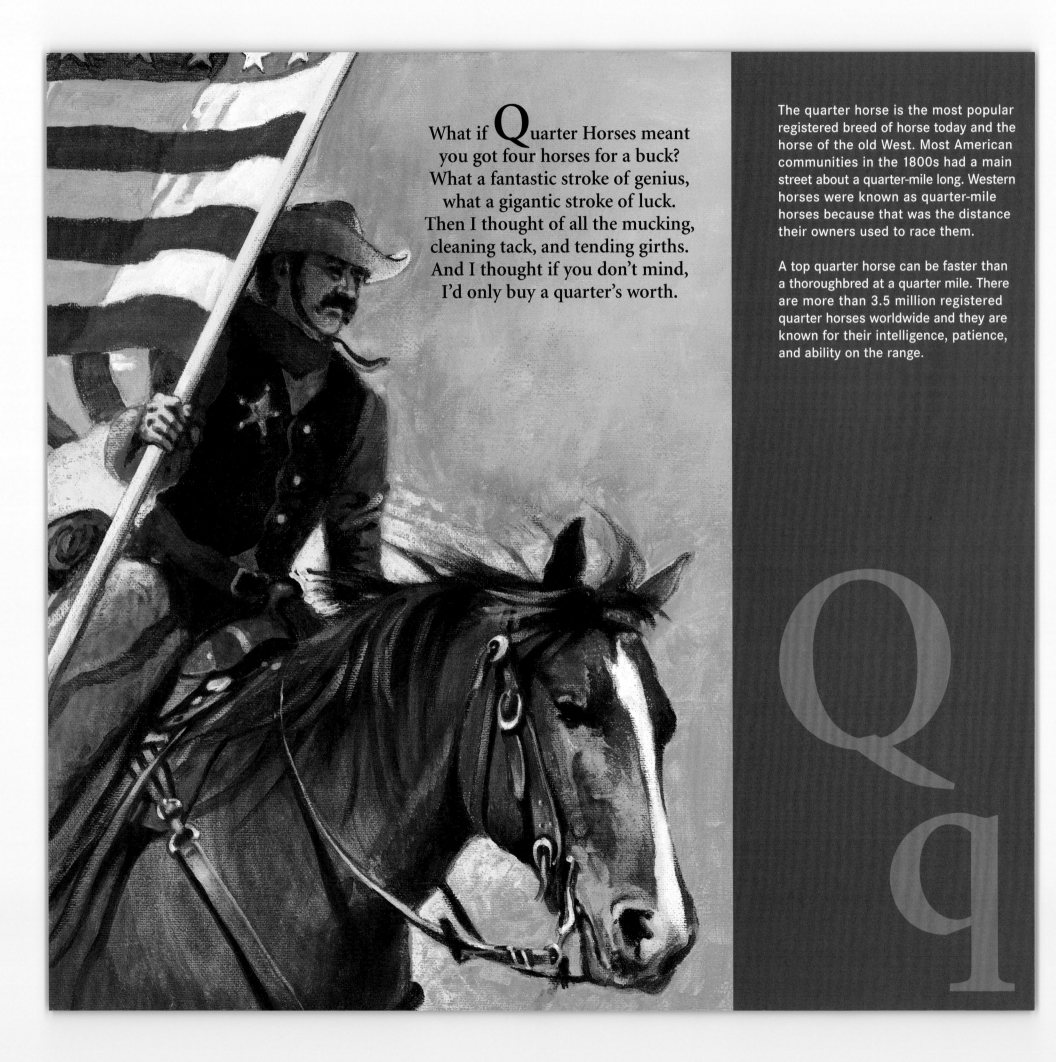

What if Quarter Horses meant
you got four horses for a buck?
What a fantastic stroke of genius,
what a gigantic stroke of luck.
Then I thought of all the mucking,
cleaning tack, and tending girths.
And I thought if you don't mind,
I'd only buy a quarter's worth.

The quarter horse is the most popular registered breed of horse today and the horse of the old West. Most American communities in the 1800s had a main street about a quarter-mile long. Western horses were known as quarter-mile horses because that was the distance their owners used to race them.

A top quarter horse can be faster than a thoroughbred at a quarter mile. There are more than 3.5 million registered quarter horses worldwide and they are known for their intelligence, patience, and ability on the range.

R **r**

In movies or on TV shows
you pulled the **R**eins and away you'd go.
But if you consider all reins the same,
there're a few more things I should explain.
In English, please note that two reins rule—
that goes for horses, dogs, or mules.
But if you're riding on the range
you just need one hand on your reins.

How you rein your horse is one of the many areas where English and Western riding differ. Cowboys needed to have a free hand for lassoing and opening and closing gates. They developed a reining style in which one hand was kept free for work. Western riders often use neck reining where a rein laid across a horse's neck indicates which way he should go.

English riders use different tack and riding techniques than Western riders. No matter what the discipline, the most important attribute a rider can bring is "soft hands." That means never pulling the horse with sharp tugs on the mouth. A good rider uses subtle shift in body position to direct her horse. Reins are used to keep the horse collected and moving with the maximum economy and comfort.

Stars, snips, and blazes are terms used to describe the markings on a horse's face. A star is any white marking between or above the eyes. A snip is a white marking between the nostrils. A blaze is a wide mark down the horse's face.

S also stands for saddles, the biggest and probably the most important piece of tack you will put on your horse. Saddles include hunt-seat, originally designed for fox hunting, dressage saddles, and western saddles, the easy chair of the American West.

Some think **S**tars are up toward heaven.
Some think Snip means hair's too long.
Some think blaze means fire a burnin'.
Some folks get these things all wrong.
Snips and stars and blaze are markings—
they make horses works of art,
and thank goodness horses have them
'cause I can't tell them apart.

Ss

Tt

A horse has basic patterns of movement: walk, trot, and gallop. In the walk, a horse puts one foot down at a time for a four-beat rhythm. In the trot, or two-beat rhythm, one front foot and its opposite rear foot hit the ground at the same time. The gallop is a three-beat rhythm with one hind leg, and then another hind leg and a front leg, and then the other front leg, hitting the ground in sequence.

T is also for temperature. One of the ways to tell if a horse is hot is to put your hand between the horse's forelegs, in the area up against his chest or under his belly. If the area feels hot, he needs to be cooled down. You should also look for heat and note how hard the horse is breathing. Warming up and cooling down is as important for a horse as it is for any athlete. It shouldn't take longer than 15 minutes of gentle walking to bring a horse's temperature down. You should also warm up a horse with a gentle walk at the beginning of a ride.

Horses have just one big omission.
They come without automatic transmission.
So then T is the start of Trot—
that's second gear, right after walk.
For many, third would have to be
what you do when cantering,
and when you're galloping with your horse
that means you've got him up to fourth.

U is for Unity.
Like a hand in a glove,
a bond that's been fostered
through time and through love.
The goal is one movement
between animal and man,
no line where one ended
and the other began.

If your horse won't eat or drink,
   if she never wants to poo,
if she's shivering or sweating,
   here's the one thing you should do:
V   Get the doc who'll make a house call;
ets are folks who always will.
He will cure your horse's problem
while your parents pay the bill.

While experienced horse people are good at treating minor injuries, calling a veterinarian when your horse appears ill or lame is the surest way to minimize damage. If your horse has a consistently high temperature, if she rolls around a great deal in her stall, if she is off her feed, call the vet. For minor injuries on the trail such as cuts or scrapes, make sure you have a first aid kit for your horse that contains bandages, eye solutions, and wraps.

V is also for vaccines. Vaccines protect a horse against tetanus, distemper, equine encephalitis, and rhinopneumonitis. Vaccinations work for horses (and people) by introducing very small doses of a disease. The body creates an antibody so when the real disease attacks the horse, the antibody is ready to fight it off. Horses need annual vaccinations, administered by a vet.

When you have the urge to read,
   an arena's really what you need.
    There are letters on the wall;
     you'll have time to read them all;
you'll spend hours just looking up
   at H and E and all such stuff.
     Don't be worried that X is gone;
      you've ridden over it all along.

Riding instructors use letters posted on arena walls to illustrate where they want their students to guide their horses. The letters give the rider a point on which to focus. Arena work is a great way to make productive use of rainy, snowy, or cold days. Some patterns you will see performed in an arena are serpentine or figure eights. While you can't see X, it is recognized as the letter in the center of the arena floor.

A sire is the father of the young.
The dam is where the baby came from.
For the first five months or so
mares carry kitchens for their foals.
Weanlings have changed their favorite snacks
Y   from something in milk to something in grass.
stands for Yearling, a term that's used
for horses that are between one and two.

Y y

Z
z

Horses can indeed sleep while standing up. While they doze, their legs are locked in place to keep them standing. A horse's best sleep comes when he is lying down. Most horses will only lie down in a place in which they do not feel threatened or in the company of a trusted herd mate. Adult horses generally do not need as much sleep as people; four or five hours is usually plenty.

I envy things about my horse,
                  like how he takes his Zs—
he doesn't bother to lie down;
it makes great sense to me.
If I could sleep just like my horse
           and doze while sitting up,
I'd volunteer to play left field
      and stand through algebra.

Mike Ulmer

Mike Ulmer is a father of three females and the guardian of another, Criquet, a three-year-old Paso Fino who was born in Georgia. He caught the horse bug while on a family trail ride through the Lake Louise region of Alberta, Canada. This is his first book about horses. When he isn't on the trail near his home in Hamilton, Ontario, Canada, Mike writes a sports column for the *Toronto Sun* newspaper. He has written four best-selling books about hockey and a children's book, *M is for Maple: A Canadian Alphabet*. Mike is married to journalist Agnes Bongers. Their oldest daughter Sadie is an even bigger horse nut than her dad. Hannah, the middle daughter, prefers basketball to horseplay, while young Madalyn hasn't quite made up her mind.

Gijsbert van Frankenhuyzen

With the publication of *The Legend of Sleeping Bear* in 1998, illustrator Gijsbert van Frankenhuyzen fulfilled his lifelong dream to become a children's book illustrator. In addition to his many legend books with Sleeping Bear Press, other award-winning titles include *The Edmund Fitzgerald: Song of the Bell, Jam & Jelly by Holly & Nellie, Adopted by an Owl,* and *Saving Samantha.*

Gijsbert is extremely honored to have a painting from his books *Adopted by an Owl* and *The Legend of the Teddy Bear* in the permanent collection of the MAZZA Museum, at the University of Findlay, Ohio. MAZZA is dedicated to promoting literacy by providing educational programs for children and adults through children's books.

Gijsbert visits schools throughout the Great Lakes region sharing his love of art and nature. You can visit Gijsbert, his family and their animals on their web site at http://my.voyager.net/robbyn.